Psalms That Sing
Studies in the Psalms

by
T. Franklin Miller

Publication Board
of the Church of God
Warner Press
Anderson, Indiana

Contents

Chapter	Page
Introduction	v
1. Psalm 1: The Person God Blesses	11
2. Psalm 8: What Is Man?	15
3. Psalm 19: The Heavens Declare God's Glory	23
4. Psalm 23: God's Care and Protection	31
5. Psalm 40: Deliverance and Song of the Redeemed	39
6. Psalm 46: Refuge and Strength of God	47
7. Psalm 51: Cry of Repentance	55
8. Psalm 73: Worship as a Solution to Life's Problems	63
9. Psalm 84: Loveliness of God's Dwelling Place	71
10. Psalm 91: Blessings of the One Who Trusts in God	79

11. Psalm 103:
A Hymn of Thanksgiving 87
12. Psalm 119:
God's Word as Light and Life 95
13. Psalm 130:
A Song of Ascent 103

Introduction

Can you think of a hymn composed in the last twenty-five years that you believe people will still be singing one hundred years from now? Some of today's music might last that long—but probably not much of it. In these studies we are going to be reviewing hymns written not twenty-five years ago, but some of them more than three thousand years ago. They are used today in worship services in nearly every nation and in a wide variety of settings.

How remarkable that these hymns of the ancient Hebrews have persisted across the centuries and that they still speak with meaning, relevance, and encouragement to people everywhere.

The psalms probably were sung and memorized long before they were written down. They came from people of an obscure little nation with a unique faith in God. Who would have thought that a song composed by a shepherd in that little country centuries ago would so endure that millions would still derive courage, hope, and inspiration from it!

Consider some vast differences between the two worlds—then and now. The psalms were composed by rural people—even their cities would be villages by today's standards; we are urban and suburban. Many of them were simple, nomadic herdsmen; we are sophisticated, highly literate, and a part of an industrial society. They were a tightly knit religious culture; today's Christians span the gamut from "free worship" to liturgical, rich and poor, across all social, cultural, economic, and ethnic backgrounds. The psalms have lived on and on, speaking their messages to every age and every generation.

The psalms are universal in appeal because they deal with universal needs and hungers and experiences. Every generation has to face these questions: Who am I? Where did I come from? Where am I going? What is the meaning of life? Who is God? Why do people suffer? Why do the wicked seem to prosper? Who cares for me? Where do I find hope in my despair? What are the purposes of the Creator of the universe?

As we examine just a few of these great psalms in some detail, let us try to discover what has made them enduring and universal in appeal.

Hebrew Poetry

A few reminders of the nature of Hebrew

poetry may help in a clearer understanding of the psalms.

The psalms come to us in poetic form partly because they were to be recited and sung to the accompaniment of musical instruments. While much of the poetic expression is lost in the translations, even in the English versions we feel the rhythm, cadences, and vivid imagery. Hebrew poetry does not depend on rhyme; nor is there a strong effort for it to fall into carefully measured stanzas.

A strong characteristic is parallelism. The first line is balanced by a corresponding line that further illuminates. Sometimes the second line repeats the first in slightly different words, as in Psalm 19:1—"How clearly the sky reveals God's glory! How plainly it shows what he has done!" In another kind of parallelism the second line completes the meaning, as in 146:2—"I will praise him as long as I live; I will sing to my God all my life." A third kind of parallelism is called ascending, as in Psalm 24:7-8—"Fling wide the gates, open the ancient doors, and the great king will come in! Who is this great king? He is the Lord, strong and mighty, the Lord, victorious in battle!" A fourth kind of parallelism is called contrasting, as illustrated by Psalm 1:6—"The righteous are guided and protected by the Lord, but the evil are on the way to their doom." Our study of the Psalms will be enriched by our recognition of this characteristic.

The Language of Worship

A few of the psalms may be thought of as almost totally individual in nature, but for the most part they are the literature of the worshiping community. Many, in fact, cannot be understood outside the setting of a congregation at worship. Sometimes the words were to be said or chanted by the priest or sometimes a soloist. Often the choir gave response, and usually the entire congregation joined in the chanting or singing or repetition of certain refrains or responses.

The psalms depend greatly on figures of speech and on symbolic language to express feelings, hopes, fears, aspirations, and experiences common to all people everywhere. They are rich in comparison, exaggeration, and other imageries. One kind of comparison used is simile, in which one thing is said to be like another. Psalm 103:13, for example, says, "As a father is kind to his children, so the Lord is kind to those who honor him." In metaphor, one thing is simply said to be another, as in Psalm 23: "The Lord is my shepherd." A picturesque exaggeration is found in Psalm 6:6: "Every night I flood my bed with tears" (RSV). Many other word pictures will delight you as you read the Psalms.

The psalms grew out of the lives, trials, struggles, and victories of the Hebrew people across a period of several hundred years. They speak of deliverance, personal communion with God, thanksgiving for his goodness and gifts, and a sense of a special Hebrew heritage. They apparently circulated in smaller collections before being brought together in their present form. About half the psalms are associated with David, but other names appear at the headings of many poems (for example, Solomon with Psalm 72, and Moses with Psalm 90).

The psalms are categorized in various ways. We find in them hymns of praise, prayers in time of crisis, and songs of faith. Another look at their contents finds nature psalms, praise to the Lord of history, songs of Zion, personal supplications, penitential prayers, psalms of thanksgiving, laments, psalms of trust, psalms of wisdom and communion.

Psalm 1 may be thought of as introductory to the entire collection, and Psalm 150 the culmination, summary, and postlude. Some of these psalms go back to a thousand years or more before Christ, and, as we shall see, were designed to serve different functions. Yet what remarkable unity there is, starting with chapter 1 and going all the way to 150!

Their use in all Hebrew worship for some three thousand years, and in all Christian worship for almost two thousand years, places them in a unique position among religious literature and music.

Chapter 1
The Person God Blesses
Psalm 1

Psalm 1 exalts the Law of God (the Torah to the Hebrew people). It would be interesting to compare this psalm with the Beatitudes of Jesus in the Sermon on the Mount (Matthew 5 ff). In this case, the word *blessed*, or *happy*, has its roots in the idea of one going forth, one advancing, one leading the way. Truly the happy person is one who leads the way or opens a path to worship, service, witness, fellowship, and study of the Word of God.

As the term is often used in the Bible, happiness is not a self-centered emotion or a static situation. The happy person is possessed with a dynamic faith that compels one to advance into areas of witness, service, and meeting of human need.

The simile used is one familiar to people living in Palestine. A tree needs water if it is to grow and produce fruit. So this blessed person—the one who meditates on and obeys God's Word—is like a tree planted close to water where it will grow and develop and bear

11

fruit. Could it be that some "barren" Christians have little fruit of the Spirit because they do not study and meditate on the Word of God, or because they are not obedient to God's will?

The Person Who Perishes

The first word of this psalm is blessed and the last word is *perish*. Blessedness comes from obedience to God and following God's Word. The disobedient have no alternative—they perish.

Consider the description of the obedient and happy person in verses one through three and then notice the contrast of the disobedient and unhappy person in verses four and five. It becomes clear that the psalm is referring to people who are poles apart by their own choices and decisions.

Whereas the obedient servant is like a growing, fruitful tree, the disobedient is like the chaff. This figure of speech is from the rural setting of the farmer who used primitive methods to separate grain from straw, or chaff. After the grain was harvested and the stalks were broken and softened, the farmer would toss some grain into the air; the good grain would fall to the threshing floor to be gathered for food, but the wind would blow away the chaff and dust and dry straw. Thus the disobedient servant is portrayed as worthless, making no lasting contribution for good.

The living tree is permanent, enduring, and fruitful. The chaff is wasted, gone with the wind, to be lost and forgotten.

Are We Trees or Chaff?

The lesson is clear for us. Each person, each family, each community, each nation faces the alternative ways of living. We are the sad witnesses of many who have chosen the path of disobedience, and the empty chaff of their lives is a mockery of what might have been otherwise fruitful stewardship of God-given resources. The illustrations are on every television newscast, in every newspaper—and there are thousands that did not make headlines—immorality, corruption in government, unethical business and professional life, loose living, and decay in morals and ethics and values.

The persons who do not usually make the headlines are those who live by goodness, integrity, honesty, fruitfulness, giving a full day of good work for a day's pay, love, forgiveness, serving others.

Here are the two ways. We all make our own choices, and then we live with the consequences of our decisions.

Some Guidelines for Further Study

These studies are based in large part on *Good News for Modern Man* (Today's English Version). Each member should be encouraged to have a copy to mark significant passages as he or she reads. Some will prefer other versions. A paraphrase will sometimes open a new window of understanding, but it may be a long way from the original Scriptures. If you use a paraphrase, why not ask members to write their own paraphrases of this psalm?

Remember that Psalm 1 introduces the whole book. Praising God for his mighty acts in history, meditating on the Law, and seeking to know and to do God's will, are really what the psalm is all about.

Finally, read the psalm in unison, if possible, and reinforce the idea that each of us chooses to be either a fruitful tree or dry straw, obedient and happy as servants of God or rebellious and lost to God's purpose.

Chapter 2
What Is Man?
Psalm 8

Thirty centuries or more separate two men who had the same idea. One was a nomadic Hebrew in rough clothing of goatskin or camel's hair, never traveling more than a hundred miles or so from the place where he was born, a herdsman with time for reflection on life and its meaning, living in the most primitive condition. The other wore a space suit, had just been shot into space to orbit the earth in a space ship equipped with fantastic, unimaginable, sophisticated controls and means of communication. Yet astronaut John Glenn was moved to quote the ancient psalmist as he considered the heavens, the stars, the creator of it all, and the nature of humankind, the created.

The opening and closing words of this psalm are identical:

"Lord, our Lord, your greatness is seen in all the world!"

It is likely that for centuries this psalm was used as a hymn of praise, the congregation singing with reverence, awe, and wonder their sense of the majesty of God. The feelings out-distance the words. No language expresses adequately the wonder of God's created universe—whether seen by the Hebrew in the still, clear night under the Oriental sky, or by an astronaut gliding at fantastic speed through the vastness of space, looking down at this small planet called Earth. Words fail to express the grandeur and majesty of God. The heart bursts forth in song.

Verses 3 to 8 may have been sung by a solo voice; a voice inspired by these lofty thoughts of God's creation could surely lift the worshiping congregation to the height of reverence. Can you imagine how you would respond if you were a part of that throng that was praising God when a clear tenor or soprano voice burst forth in joy, exultation, gratitude, and wonder!

After the solo, the congregation would again repeat the refrain, perhaps chanting in reverence the same words that opened the hymn. Small wonder that such a hymn of praise has endeared itself to three thousand years of men and women who found it an expression of their own wonder, awe, and praise.

As we consider the mysteries of God's created universe, either the tiniest atom or the expanding horizons of space exploration, we may in humility bow anew before our Creator. We may yield to a new sense of reverence and find renewed purpose in the life God has given us. Can we believe, also, that the God of the vast universe is also concerned about each of us and is at the very center of the struggle we all find in our hearts?

The Insignificance of Human Beings

When the singer turns to the majesty and glory of God, human beings seem small and unimportant. The contrast between God's greatness and human frailty is overwhelming indeed!

This idea of our insignificance is not foreign to our age, and it has crept into the thinking of people of all the centuries. Sometimes we feel that one person is so tiny and fragile in this world and that the earth is so small among the whirling planets and distant stars. People may seem very small as measured against the forces of nature, for what can they do to change the seasons, end a drought, stop an earthquake, soothe a tornado, or dry up the monsoon rains or raging floods?

Is a person only a mere speck of protoplasm in this vast universe of unimagined power and space and distance? Theodore Roosevelt is said to have periodically walked out onto his porch late at night to contemplate the stars in order to remind himself of his proper place in the universe.

Even in our own order, our own society, it often seems that one mere person can do nothing—absolutely nothing—to change the course of events. This is one view of humanity, which can result from doing just what this singer did—*consider* the created universe. It may lead to pessimism and futility.

The Significance of Persons

But the singer does not end his hymn on a note of pessimism. He goes beyond superficial appearances to see the real worth of a person, any person. For we are created in the image of God. We are made to have fellowship with God. We are not equal with God. But neither are we merely animal. We have dominion over all things, a power *granted* to us by God.

So of all created beings, a person is the only one who can stand up to God and say yes or no. We alone can make moral choices. Only we can discriminate between good and evil. Only we can be held accountable to God as stewards over all other created beings.

One person is of uncounted worth. One person does make a difference. One person—with God—can always change the path of history. Isn't this one of the great truths revealed in the Bible and in all human history, that one person surrendered to the power of God can be pitted against the whole stream of society and can be a change-agent in the hands of God?

The Community of Worship

Gazing into the starry skies, we marvel at the universe and the creator behind it, but we quickly realize that the responsibility God gave us as individuals exists within the community

God has brought into being. This sense of corporate worship appears more clearly in other psalms than in this one. Within the congregation or the worshiping body we find the door to true worship; we join with others in praising God and in responding to God's call to service.

Can Dominion Be Trusted?

Most religions in the ancient world held that the gods were natural powers and that human life with its rhythmic cycles of fertility was somehow caught up in this mysterious relationship with nature. Psalm 8 declares differently. God is not a natural power but maker and sustainer of all persons and is supernatural. As creator he has commissioned persons, his highest created beings, to be his representatives, or stewards, to have dominion over all else God has created. Think of the way this concept has affected our development in such fields as education, transportation, medicine, communication, concern for human welfare, conservation of natural resources. What responsibility God has entrusted to us!

Also, what a risk God has taken! In placing people in this position of power and honor, is it possible that their lordship over natural resources will tempt them to assume the role of God? This is precisely what has happened so many times and has led to warfare, chaos, enmity, despoiling of resources, depletion of energy, and exploitation of others for the benefit of a few. Yet this is a risk God has taken.

Here is a central theme of the entire Bible: humankind's high possibility and their low achievement, their grandeur and misery, their use or misuse of the tremendous power God has entrusted to them. What has this to say to our own day? Will we rise to the capability of one created "a little lower than the angels," or will humanity sink to the level of the beast in the jungle?

Notes on the Biblical Text

"Our Lord" (8:1). In the Hebrew custom a name not only designates, it contains the nature of that for which it is named. The Lord's character is glory, majesty, an authoritative presence that fills the whole earth.

"Heavens . . . , children . . . , babies" (8:1-2). The whole creation, even babies and children, sings spontaneous hymns of praise to God, whose glory is evident in both his handiwork and his power to defeat the forces of evil.

"Look at the sky" (8:3). There were no blinding city lights, no heavy smog to obscure the clear vision of the poet who contemplated the starry night heavens. It has been suggested that this psalm is a hymn to be sung out of doors at night.

"Inferior only to yourself" (8:5-8). Humankind have been given both honor and responsibility over all God has created.

"What is man?" (8:4). Those who today are puzzled by this question would do well to accept the songwriter's answer. We are God's creation, made in the image of God, highest of all created beings, small and insignificant compared with the vastness of the universe, yet endowed by God with stewardship responsibilities for developing all these resources. Each individual is of inestimable value.

"Our Lord" (8:9). Such contemplation should lead to humility, reverence, and awe. It should inspire truer worship and adoration of God.

Some Guidelines for Further Study

Perhaps this week families or small groups could have a brief worship experience out of doors at night. Spend some time stargazing in meditation. Using flashlights, read the entire psalm together. Or let the group sing "Praise God from Whom All Blessings Flow"; then let one person read verses 3 through 8 slowly, and finish with the group responding with the same doxology.

Discuss some of the various ideas of what humanity is and the influence of these ideas on society. For example: Are we high animals whose appetites are to be satisfied in any way possible? Hitler said the human was born to die for the state; consider the implications of that philosophy.

Discuss the use and misuse of the power God has given us. This may lead to consideration of disregard for spoilage or depletion of many natural resources. It may lead to discussion of political and social power. How should power be used?

Discuss how some persons have allowed power to overcome their sense of stewardship and have assumed the role of gods themselves.

What has modern space exploration and related technology added to our concept of the majesty of the Creator and the stewardship accountability of people given "dominion" by God?

Chapter 3
The Heavens Declare God's Glory

Psalm 19

There is a popular idea that David is the author of all the psalms. Although he did not write all of them, Psalm 19 is called "a psalm of David" and is dedicated to the choir-master. Almost half of the psalms probably were written by David or inspired by him. Others are attributed to the choir leader Asaph, to the sons of Korah, to Moses, to Solomon, to Heman, and to Ethan. To the people of Israel, ascribing a psalm to David did not necessarily mean he was its author, but it did mean that when the community came to worship God the psalms they sang were identified with David.

Some psalms were written for special occasions, notably for Hebrew festivals, the celebration of the new year, or the coronation of the king; several were processional chants for approaching the temple. Some are individual hymns of praise or of lament. Some are for the entire congregation. Many are hymns of the majesty of God. Some are liturgies with responses by congregation, choir, or priest.

Three in One

Psalm 19 appears to be three hymns in one chapter. First it is a hymn to the creator of the universe and is not unlike Psalm 8 in some respects. Next is a meditation on the law of God. Last, there is a personal prayer. All three parts are worthy of our careful study.

The Heavens Are Telling

Hebrew thought embraced three realms of existence: heaven, the highest; Sheol, the lowest; and the land of the living in between. Sheol, place of the dead, is silent. Human beings on earth can sing praise to God if they are so inclined. But in heaven everything is continually praising God. The faithful and obedient followers of God will join the heavenly choirs in their anthems of praise.

Anyone who has ever listened to a full massed choir singing "The Heavens Are Telling" from *The Creation* by Haydn could never doubt the intensity of feeling that bursts forth in Psalm 19. Joseph Haydn composed his famous oratorio, his crowning masterpiece, when he was sixty-five years old after he had returned to his native Austria from London where he had brought out his famous twelve London symphonies. One of the most inspired moments of your life would be to listen, with exultation and reverence, to "The Heavens Are Telling."

We often turn to the wonders of creation as

24

proof or evidence of God. But the Hebrews did not start where we so often do. The faith of Israel was grounded in the history of divine deliverance. When everything pointed to the impossible, from a human point of view, God granted deliverance and unveiled himself in many other miraculous events. So the praise from the world of nature is simply enhancing the praise of Israel. They started with faith in God because of their experiences in history, and joyful, exultant praise was the result.

Does this happen to us? Do we take time to recall the wondrous and marvelous events of God's mighty acts in history? When we do, nothing can prevent us from joining the heavenly chorus in joyous praise of the God who alone is worthy of our worship.

The Law of the Lord

Just as the first section of this psalm has inspired breath-taking beauty in music across the centuries, so this second part is a literary masterpiece. This hymn is in praise of the Law (Torah).

People of faith thus do see in nature evidences of God's handiwork, but it is in this inspired Word that he is best known by the believing and obedient community. We know that Jesus so regarded the Old Testament, including the Law, the Prophets, and the Wisdom Literature. The early Christians maintained this attitude toward the revealed Word of God, going beyond only to witness that in Jesus Christ himself had God perfectly revealed himself.

God, who created the world and has filled it with evidences of his glorious handiwork, has given to his covenant people a way of life that is far more majestic than the display of power and glory in the natural universe.

A Prayer for Humility and Guidance

Meditating on the world God has made and studying his Word always humbles us. He calls us to self-examination. We are made aware of the subtle temptations of pride and arrogance and of gradually assuming that we are the measure of all things. The foundation of our faith is not in what we have done or can do, but rather in what God has given and done.

In the presence of the holy God the psalmist examines his own ambitions, desires, thoughts, and actions. He does not compare himself with other people; nor is he content to do just a little bit better than the average person he knows. He is measuring himself against God and the Law. That is the test of real religion. It is the test of everyone who aspires to please God.

The closing verse is often quoted in our own prayers today or sung by choir or congregation as part of divine worship. When sung or prayed sincerely and honestly, what greater prayer could there be?

So with these three parts put together, Psalm

19 stands as one of the great passages in this ancient hymnal, men and women the world over still sing and pray it.

Notes on the Biblical Text

"The sky reveals . . . and . . . announces" (19:1-2). This part of the psalm was perhaps originally a part of the new year festival when a prominent theme was celebrating God as creator. We should remember that this is Oriental poetry, with a great amount of symbolism and imagery. These verses reflect the world view of that period of time, which seemed to attribute to all objects of nature their awareness and knowledge that they were created by God.

"No speech . . . no sound" (19:3). The anthem of the heavens is beyond the limitations of human language. All people understand it as they experience reverence, awe, mystery, and wonder in beholding the created universe, especially as they consider the heavens. Everybody can see the stars, sun, moon; everyone can see light and experience darkness—wordless wonders.

"The sun" (19:4-6). Two figures of speech are used to refer to the sun: *bridegroom* and *athlete*. We remember, of course, that when this was written, earth was thought to be flat, not round. The sun, not the earth, was thought to move. (We still speak of the sun's coming up and going down.) The chief difference here between Babylonian paganism and Hebrew the-

27

ology is that the pagans made the *sun itself a god;* the Hebrew poet saw the sun as a part of the creation of the one true God.

"The law of the Lord" (19:7-11). This passage is one of the Torah hymns. We have looked briefly at another, Psalm 1, and will consider another later when we examine the lengthy Psalm 119, which is praise to God for giving this expression of his will and purpose. If the Torah meant so much to the ancient Hebrew, how much more should the whole Bible mean to the Christian today!

Each line in this stanza uses a distinctive word for the Law and suggests what that accomplishes in the life of the obedient follower.

The words referring to the Torah are (a) law, (b) commands, (c) rules, (d) commandments, (e) worship, (f) judgments (as used in Today's English Version).

The Law is thus described as (a) perfect, (b) trustworthy, (c) right, (d) completely just, (e) good, (f) fair, (g) desirable, and (h) sweeter than honey.

The benefits that result are (a) new life, (b) wisdom to those who need it, (c) happiness to the obedient, (d) understanding, (e) endurance, (f) satisfaction.

So the Law brings refreshment and renewal to the spirit, wisdom to the humble, joy to the heart, understanding to the mind, an awareness of a deep, abiding, and dependable security to the obedient servant.

"Deliver me" (19:12-13). Here is an honest poet. He freely admits his imperfections and frailties. He knows of errors and mistakes. He confesses sin in his life, but he is grateful for the constant forgiveness of God. He acknowledges how easy it is to become proud and presumptuous, to rebel against God, to run his own life the way he pleases without regard to the will of God. His prayer is that God will prevent this arrogance.

"The meditation of my heart" (19:14, RSV). The meaning of the word *meditation* here is something that one thinks about night and day, to ponder and consider, even as John Paterson says, to keep "humming its words under his breath."

Some Guidelines for Study

Today's English Version does not give titles to individual psalms, but many other versions do. Using such a version, list the titles of various psalms and note the occasion or event they celebrate and to whom they are ascribed.

Ask three different persons or groups to read aloud the three parts of this psalm and observe the differences in purpose and content.

Try reading this psalm aloud once or twice each day for a week, each time praying sincerely the prayer in verse 14. Write down at the close of each day some of your own thoughts (meditations) or actions that you feel might not be acceptable to God.

As you study the poem on the Torah (19:7-10), what additional words could you add that would further describe the nature and results of obedience to the Word of God? Test each day by asking whether today's offering to God—time, talent, imagination, prayer, worship, service—is an acceptable offering to him.

Chapter 4
God's Care and Protection
Psalm 23

Here is the best known and surely most loved of all the psalms. Most of us learned it as children, we repeat it often in unison with the worshiping congregation, and we use it in weddings as well as funerals and on many other occasions. In the Hebrew tradition one who made a vow or promise to God would tell the worshiping congregation of his distress or need, his release from trouble, and acknowledge with sincere gratitude God's help in his time of trouble. All of this, and more, is in Psalm 23.

God Is the Shepherd

Since the ancient Hebrews were nomadic herdsmen, the figure of a shepherd was most appropriate. Even when some settled into farms, they still kept sheep. The imagery of sheep and shepherd was the best one available to describe one's complete dependence upon God, his care, concern, and trustworthiness.

Although modern people are far removed from the ancient wandering shepherd caring for his sheep, the central message of this great chapter still speaks with relevance and meaning to our deepest needs.

God Cares for His People

Both Old and New Testaments keep central the fundamental faith that God loves his people, cares for them, and is concerned for their welfare. This message was proclaimed by both patriarchs and prophets through the long history of God's dealings with his covenant people.

Jesus emphasized so often God's care and concern for his children and how this care and concern should call them to live in obedience and faith. Not a sparrow falls to the ground unnoticed by God, and each person is worth infinitely more than many sparrows. The smallest detail of life is his concern, as indicated in the figure of speech about numbering the hairs of the head. Wild flowers blooming profusely, untended, on the hillside are reminders that we can trust the Good Shepherd to care for all our needs. We can affirm with Paul, "My God will supply all your needs" (Phil. 4:19), and with the psalmist we can know that with God as shepherd we shall not want.

God Is Our Guide

For their safety and well-being, sheep need a shepherd to guide them, to lead them where their needs can be met and they can be safe.

The Good Shepherd is also *our* guide. In dark valleys or by clear waters he always works redemptively. He is present to guide in every situation. For each of us and for all of us he has a plan. Our salvation comes when we cooperate with him in the fulfillment of that plan and our own moral and spiritual redemption.

Even when we, like sheep, wander astray, the Shepherd seeks and guides us back to the right path. When we deviate, by accident or by choice or by ignorance, God still is at work redemptively for our good. Dr. Leslie Weatherhead, first as pastor of City Temple Church in London and later in a widely read book, made clear how God seeks his will for our lives—or attempts to guide us. Weatherhead referred to the ultimate or perfect will, which most of us never achieve; the intentional will; and the circumstantial will. When we, for any of many reasons, fail to follow his guidance and wander into sin, error, trouble, and difficult circumstances, he still has a will at work for our good. Perhaps the *best* has been forfeited, and yet he still works in all circumstances for our *good*. The Shepherd will not let us continue to wander into paths of evil and trouble without seeking to guide us back to a better way.

God Is Our Renewal

The need to have one's soul restored or renewed is universal. All of us have experienced the futility and fatigue that we describe as the end of the rope. An athlete knows this. He or she plays until another step cannot be taken; but the athlete does take it, and he or she gets what is called a second wind. New vigor and strength surge in to make the athlete a winner.

So it is with all of us. God is the one who brings us the second wind, the second chance, renewal of hope, restoration of courage and faith. Isaiah referred to the restoring of one's soul as the renewal of strength, and he said it came by waiting upon the Lord, and by complete surrender to the will of God. (See Isaiah 40:28-31.)

Restoring of the soul may come in different ways, but central in all of them is worship, surrender, and obedience to God. It may come in times of personal or congregational worship and prayer. Many find it in the honesty and concern of a small group that is a redemptive fellowship of divine love. It comes to all who in quiet hospitality open the door of heart and mind and let the peace of God, beyond all understanding, bring new perspective, renewal of strength, and restoration of soul.

God Is Our Guard

Just as the sheep fear no evil because of the protection of the shepherd, so we can trust God to guard us. We should be careful, though, not to assume that because we are obedient servants of God we will avoid all pain or trouble. God does not promise that. We are not promised ease or success or freedom from pain, trouble, or sorrow.

This must have been a difficult dilemma for some of the Hebrews, for they were often bothered that the wicked seemed to prosper and the righteous often suffered. It is still bothersome to many Christians. But the important fact to remember is that we are promised the presence of God, and in his presence we do not need to fear the evil or trouble or calamity that come our way. He has promised that he will provide courage and hope and strength. He has promised that the enemies will not overcome, for ultimate victory belongs to God. In the midst of adversity he gives courage and the ability to face every situation with confident hope.

A Simple Shepherd Story

In his booklet titled *The Song of Our Syrian Guest*, W. A. Knight refers to an Oriental custom that might illuminate this psalm further. As the sheep return to the fold at the close of the day, the shepherd stands at the opening and is himself the door. He holds back each sheep while he looks it over for injuries. Olive oil, which is carried in a horn, is placed on a bruise or severe scratch. Additional medication, such as cedar tar, might be used for severe injury. The shepherd dips his large, two-handled cup into the container of water, and the sheep may drink cool water from a cup literally running over. A sheep that is overly tired might find the shepherd rubbing olive oil over its face and head, then splashing cool water over its body. Into the safety of the sheepfold it goes to rest, assured that the shepherd will always take good care of it.

Notes on the Biblical Text

"The Lord" (23:1). While the Old Testament frequently portrays God as the Shepherd and Israel his sheep, this psalm begins with a personal testimony—"my shepherd." Can we say that, too?

"He lets me rest" (23:2). The shepherd knows where the good pasture is and leads the sheep to it. When they have eaten enough, he leads them to water and a place to rest. Without this leadership, the sheep could overeat, wander into danger, and become ill or die. Many versions state, "He makes me lie down." That is a helpful word for those who because of illness or other adversity are forced to inactivity; that in itself could be a time of inward renewal.

"He gives me new strength" (23:3). Rest brings renewal, and when the sheep are ready for grazing or travel, the shepherd leads onward.

"Through deepest darkness" (23:4). In Palestine the brilliant sunshine could form dark shadows in valleys or under overhanging cliffs; wild animals might lurk in the shadows; the shepherd must be ever watchful. The rod might be used as a club, sometimes studded with rock-like spikes, for defense. The staff, or shepherd's crook, would steer a straying sheep or pull it back from danger.

"You prepare a banquet" (23:5). The law of the desert provided refuge for anyone pursued by enemies. When the person came to a tent, the owner was obligated to give the fugitive safety. His host, though a total stranger, was obligated to feed him, even though his enemies might be sitting just outside. For two days and one night the fugitive was guaranteed food, shelter, safety—a custom well known to all Hebrews.

"My home as long as I live" (23:6). Here the figure of speech changes, and as a sheep knows it will not be without the protection of the good shepherd, so the poet sings a testimony that the length of his days will be in God's care.

Some Guidelines for Further Study

Perhaps you could begin this session by having the class repeat, in unison, the Twenty-third Psalm from the King James Version. Then have it read from several other versions, including Today's English Version.

Ask for class members to share memories of times when this psalm had special meaning for them.

Discuss some of the reasons why a poem so short, sung by nomadic, desert-dwelling shepherds centuries ago, has such profound meaning to so many of us in a society so totally different—urban, sophisticated, affluent, educated—as well as to persons in other situations.

Ask the members for their own interpretations and understandings of these different passages and figures of speech.

You might ask someone to read to the class Jesus' reference to sheep and shepherd as recorded in John 10:1-16. Note the many similarities to Psalm 23.

Chapter 5
Deliverance and Song of the Redeemed

Psalm 40

Many of the psalms are hymns of thanksgiving to God, praising him for his goodness. Some are individual and some congregational. Many others have been classified as laments, again some individual and some congregational. The term *lament* to us may suggest a mood of depression or a pessimistic outlook, but in the psalms laments are concerned with taking adversity to God, who has power over all. Psalm 40 contains a hymn of thanksgiving (vv. 1-11) and a lament (vv. 12-17). Verses 13-17 parallel Psalm 70.

A Cry for Help

Who of us today cannot identify with the poet who, in deep distress, cried to God for help? The reference to the dangerous pit, or Sheol, seems to imply that he was near death. Whatever it was, his adversity was intense. He was in deep distress and he prayed; God heard and answered—thanks be to God!

Sheol, or the underworld, was the abode of the dead, and this man felt he was close to it. In the slippery mud, such as the bottom of a deep well, no firm foothold could be found; but when he prayed, God lifted him up to a solid rock. What is our usual reaction in time of real difficulty? Do we turn to God in earnest prayer? Do we call to mind the words of Jesus that, instead of fainting in despair, we should always pray?

God Gives a New Song

True religion always begins with acknowledging what God has done. All through the psalms the foundation of faith is not in who we are or what we have done, but always in what God has given and done. Today so much religious emphasis is on human achievement, on self-realization, on aspiration, and using one's own resources. This is the opposite of the biblical view of religion made so clear in the Psalms.

In this case, the poet might have elaborated on his suffering or compared his troubles with those of other people. Instead of that, he keeps God at the center and expresses that all he is and has become he owes to the mercy and kindness and goodness of God.

Even to those of us who really cannot sing very well, God gives a *new* song. In the New Testament, under the Christian faith, this being lifted up from the depths and slippery footing to solid rock is like a new birth—in fact, it is a birth of new life. And with that comes joy, praise, exultation, and a new perspective on life.

A Call to Remembrance

The poet now calls upon the congregation to remember the way God has dealt with Israel across the years. He cannot speak of all God has done for the good of this covenant people. The recounting of God's acts of power in saving Israel was one big factor in keeping them together. The story was told over and over with dramatic effect, from father to children, to the congregation.

Do we give as much thought to whence we came and how divine mercy and kindness have operated in our lives? Do we tell others what God has done for us? Do we take for granted the goodness of the Heavenly Father? How much time do we take in praising God for giving deliverance from sin, from adversity, from trouble?

A New Insight into Sacrifice and Offering

It was the custom for one to come to the place of worship and tell of deliverance from trouble. In Jerusalem, this place would be the Temple. With this act of thanksgiving one would bring a sacrifice, maybe a dove or a lamb, to be placed upon an altar of fire and burned.

Now comes a poet with new insight into what God really wants. For primitive worshipers the burning of an offering was all right, but what God most desires is the offering of one's

41

life of love, obedience, justice, kindness, and humility. (See Micah 6:6-8 or Amos 5:21-24.)

We cannot help asking ourselves whether we are offering God what he really wants. Our time, talent, and possessions (a tithe is just the starting point) are to be given. These, however, can never substitute for moral and ethical living, a loving and forgiving attitude, bearing the fruit of the Spirit of God.

A Personal Testimony

The first part of this psalm closes with the personal testimony of the poet. He has not rejected the practice of offering a sacrifice on the altar, but he has stated that more than that is asked by God. Now he is deeply moved and tells the whole congregation the experience he has had in being saved from destruction. When the way was closed, God opened a door. When there seemed no way out of his adversity, the Lord came to his rescue.

So now he sings. Is this a solo? a chant? Will the congregation share his exuberance and join in the song? No matter—he must tell how God answered his prayer and give witness to God's righteousness, loving power, faithfulness, and goodness.

What about us? Who of us has not been in adversity and prayed to God for help? What is our impulse—to parade our troubles, or to praise God? The call is to give a testimony where it can be heard. Who of us does not have that opportunity?

A Prayer of One Falsely Accused

After an invocation, the reason and the intensity of the psalmist's need are given. Then his prayer and desire and lament intermingle and he finds peace, and the congregation is included in the prayer.

This man confesses first his sins. They are so heavy they blind him and are as uncountable as the hairs of his head. He does not stop with confession; he continues in prayer and earnestly seeks divine help. One of the marks of the psalms is persistence in prayer. Jesus also taught us to turn to God in prayer in such phrases as "pray rather than faint," "pray without ceasing," "always pray." His life and teachings call us clearly to turn to God for help, not as a *last* resort but always.

The enemies of the writer of Psalm 40 could have been persons or difficult circumstances. He asks God to defend him but to confuse and defeat his enemies. We must remember these are *pre-Christian* psalms. Several of the psalms call for God to thunder out judgment and punishment on one's enemies. Jesus, in sharp contrast, taught us to pray for them! How different his words, "Love your enemies and pray for those who persecute you" (Matt. 5:44). We ourselves are changed for the better when we can hold a forgiving attitude toward those who use us despitefully. Praying God's blessings on your enemy may actually result in his or her finally changing and becoming a staunch friend!

Notes on the Biblical Text

"I waited . . . he listened" (40:1). Waiting is not sitting serenely with folded hands. It means praying with determination and surrender to God's will and anticipating a response.

"A dangerous pit" (40:2). The pre-Christian Hebrew did not know the Christian joy of the hope of eternal life. Most of the Hebrews viewed death as the end. Dying was going to Sheol, the place of the dead, like falling into a deep pit filled with slippery clay. The figure of speech is a vivid way of saying he was almost dead.

"A new song" (40:3-5). This is God's gift, his initiative, the offer of his renewal to everyone in distress. The content of this new song is in the words that follow. He sings of God's faithfulness and integrity and rejects his own temptation to pride and arrogance. Verse 5 probably refers to the covenant renewal that took place annually. The tribes assembled in some area designated as sacred and the leader recounted the mighty acts of God in their deliverance from Egypt and his leadership until now. There was a ceremony of renewal of the covenant relationship and their vows to God.

"Sacrifices and offerings" (40:6-8). For a fuller understanding of this practice, read from Leviticus in a modern translation. The poet agrees with the teaching of the prophets later explained in greater detail in the New Testament: God wants a humble and contrite spirit, right attitudes and relationships, love and loyalty.

"The good news" (40:9-11). The new song is of salvation, obedience to the will of God, and witness to what God does.

"Save me, Lord!" (40:12-17). He deplores idol worship and those who disobey God. He rejoices in the congregation. God has saved Israel and will save him.

Some Guidelines for Further Study

You could treat this as two psalms. As you discuss verses 1-11, give opportunity for people to share briefly similar experiences. Remind the group that this psalmist did not dwell on his troubles, but thanked God in prayer.

This is a good time to let people share their prayer habits—when, where, how frequently, with whom, and so forth.

Urge the group to be a redemptive fellowship itself, to be informed of one another's needs, to support in mutual prayer, trust, and love.

Ask the group to look at verses 12-17, while one person reads Psalm 70. Explain the ceremonial or ritual nature of the Hebrew lament.

Discuss the vast changes Jesus brought to the Hebrew religion. Will the law of love suffice in every situation? Are there times when it is better to curse one's enemies than to turn the other cheek? There is a history of God's redemptive acts to recall, and we should live so that we can pray and expect God to answer.

45

Chapter 6
Refuge and Strength of God

Psalm 46

This psalm was the inspiration for Martin Luther's great hymn of the Reformation, "A Mighty Fortress Is Our God." Anyone who has ever sung that hymn with a large congregation or has heard it sung by a great and gifted choir can never forget the sheer strength of an affirmation that behind everything is the eternal God. In his presence who can be afraid? In his might and strength who can feel insecure?

We who trust in government for security, in armed might, in books and houses and secure jobs and fruitful land may well take a lesson from Psalm 46. To this writer God's presence and power are so real they overwhelm anything that can happen. This is a fortress of faith. How much we need this today! Here is a mighty affirmation of faith that no matter what happens, God still is in control and is working redemptively for his people. The psalm is arranged in three stanzas; let us look briefly at each of them.

God Is Our Security

Whenever God's people are in trouble, he is in their midst to bring courage, hope, and victory. This hymn (46:1-3) surely was sung in the annual festivals when Hebrews gathered to celebrate their covenant relationship with God. Are these words to be taken literally? Do they refer to a volcanic eruption or tremendous earthquake? Do they refer to political turmoil and revolution when strong leaders are deposed? Is the psalm using Oriental imagery and exaggerations, so common in such literature, and drawing the background too vividly? Could this refer to national calamity? Is it referring to one's personal losses, tribulation, suffering, and adversity? We really do not know, do we? But the important point is not the nature of the distress, but the fact that in it all one may feel secure in the strength of God.

Isn't it amazing how relevant to our own days are these words written so long, long ago? We have physical destruction in earthquake and flood and landslide and volcanic eruption. The horrible pictures of human suffering from such catastrophes come to us on television. We also have political upheaval and revolution. The diplomats fly to and fro from one crisis to another, trying to put out fires of hatred, war, riot, revolution. The psalm might have been written just this morning!

We also have personal disaster apart from

these other troubles. Who has not had the world come crashing down around him or her in personal tragedy, despair, sorrow, pain, broken dreams, and frustrated hopes?

The crucial question for you and me has to do with the depth of our faith in God and our trust in his dependability. We know the joy of worship in the sanctuary, but do we have deep taproots of faith that at the heart of the universe is a God who is almighty and who is able and willing to help us in every time of need? This is no call for mere bravery or show of courage; it is a call to place our trust in the God of the psalmist, the Creator, the God who Jesus said is our Father. This does get personal, doesn't it?

A Place of Serenity in the Midst of Turmoil

Stanza 2 (46:4-7) contains more poetic expression. We must remember to read it (or sing it) as poetry, not as prose. Poetic expression uses vivid imagery, and the symbols are not to be taken literally.

The poet is saying that God's presence is like water in the desert. It brings refreshment and renewal. To the nomad, water is the symbol of life itself. In God's presence the worshiper finds rivers of joy, serenity, and strength. The joy of corporate worship in the Temple comes, above all else, from realizing God's divine presence.

No turmoil or disturbance can ultimately

defeat God or his purposes. When God speaks, his voice may bring courage and peace to his people, but to the enemy, the unregenerate heart, it may bring terror.

Have we experienced this ourselves? As darkness fled when the lights came on, so have terror and fear been banished when God spoke peace. Have you known the terror of guilt and unforgiven sins? Have you been plagued with ghosts of memories you wish could be destroyed, or by guilt that is ever with you? Have you found no place to hide? Have you been at your wit's end over impossible situations? If so, then let this psalm speak to you. Surrender every situation—past, present, future; surrender guilt, sin, malice, envy, ambition— surrender *all* to him. The river of joy will flow into your heart, the city of God's dwelling place.

The Ultimate Victory Belongs to God

This ancient hymn (46:8-11) provides strength for today's battles. By pointing to God's ultimate victory it encourages those in present difficulty. We benefit by giving this poem both a personal and a social application.

The Lord has done great things. He waits to do more and is limited only by our lack of obedience. Is there anyone reading this who cannot testify to the way God has broken bows and destroyed spears in interpersonal relationships? At work, home, school, family, in intimate friendship, misunderstanding and wrong attitudes breed unhappy relationships and before we know it war has broken out. Friend is set against friend, family against family, management against employee. But when these situations are met in the spirit of Christ, the wars are stopped. Calm, honest, frank discussion, willingness to listen and to forgive, love, concern for greater causes—these break the bows and destroy the spears. Do you know this? Have you seen it happen? Are you involved in *any* situation now in which you could be obedient to God, as a blessed peacemaker, and restore peace to fractured relationships?

Socially, we have not yet outlawed war. The arms race is worse than ever. We know nobody ever wins a war, and a nuclear blast could start a chain reaction that would devastate all humankind. Yet we continue to plan for war. There is a growing "will to peace" among the nations. There is a growing conviction that our differences must be settled in ways other than brutal warfare. While we Christians are in the minority in the world, we should hope for, pray for, and work for world peace. We are not alone. Vast millions of persons of other faiths devoutly desire someone to "stop wars all over the world."

First the dream must be in the heart. We must have the vision of what earth could be under God. David Livingston said, "Castles must first be built in the air before cottages can be built on the ground." But then the dream is not enough; our efforts, singly and unitedly, with determination and perseverance, must bring the dream to reality. Like the psalmist, we take our stand believing that we serve a God big enough to create a world of peace and goodwill, a world at harmony with God. Do you believe that?

Notes on the Biblical Text

"God" (46:1). The poet uses the Hebrew term *Yah-weh*, God, meaning the God of Jacob, the God who made covenant with Israel, the creator of the universe, the one who holds in his hand all peoples, all events, all creatures, all creation.

"Shelter and strength" (46:1). The Lord of hosts is a strong shelter in trouble, and all power is his. Can we accept by faith the words of Jesus that to him is given all power in heaven and earth? Can we sing from *experience* "A Mighty Fortress is Our God?"

"If the earth is shaken" (46:2-3). Whatever cataclysmic events the poet might have envisioned, the force of the passage is not in the intensity of calamity but the assurance of faith. "We will not be afraid." How often Jesus urged us to have no fear, to be of good courage! Are we looking at the situation or the Savior?

"There is a river" (46:4). This cannot possibly apply to the earthly Jerusalem. It has no river, or at least none worth mentioning. Hezekiah's tunnel (2 Kings 20:20) was constructed to feed the spring of Gihon into the pool of Siloam, but that is hardly a river! Spiritually, though, where God is, there is all one needs for abundant living. In the will of God we find divine resources adequate for any situation.

"The Lord Almighty" (46:7). This is a refrain exalting Jehovah, the God of a covenant relationship, a profound affirmation of faith.

"Come and see" (46:8-10). Across the centuries the nothing became of worth, the impossible was done, and the miracles of God line the highways of history like hedgerows of an Indiana farm road. See what he has done already!

In this drama, we individual Christians are players on the stage, but we have seen the script, and we know the final outcome. "The kingdom of the world has become the kingdom of our Lord" (Rev. 11:15, RSV).

Some Guidelines for Further Study

It is likely that the priest or the choir sang or chanted the stanza, and the congregation the refrain. Try it that way. Let one person, or one group (men or women), read a stanza, and then have the whole group repeat the refrain, inserting it after verse 3, and again after 7 and 11. Repeat that with some vigor and enthusiasm! If it won't disturb too many others, shout it out—as the poet meant it to be!

If you cannot sing it, at least read together Luther's hymn "A Mighty Fortress Is Our God" as you study Psalm 46.

Allow time for sharing when people have found what is promised here—security and strength in God and serenity in time of turmoil and trouble.

Chapter 7
Cry of Repentance
Psalm 51

This psalm is based on David's repentance after the prophet Nathan had confronted him about his act of adultery with Bathsheba and the murder of her husband. It is one of the very few penitential psalms and is an individual lament.

You are surely familiar with the story. King David had seen a beautiful woman, Bathsheba, bathing on a nearby housetop, and he committed adultery with her. Her husband was serving in the army, and the king tried to use him to cover up the act of sin. David then sent him to the front of the battle where he was sure to be killed. Later the prophet faced David with the sinfulness of his behavior.

The word *sin* is often used to refer to crimes, violation of law, or the breaking of a moral or ethical code. Without taking away the sense of wrong from such actions, the true nature of sin is rebellion against God or, as in the Garden of Eden, to try to become "like gods" (Gen. 3:5). This psalm shows remarkable insight: sin breaks relationship with God, setting oneself up as a god, and sinful deeds are the result. This broken fellowship with God cannot be endured; it is the same as death, for life has no meaning. The spiritual vision revealed in this psalm could rival Paul's Roman Epistle in perception of sin, confession, forgiveness, and fellowship with God. It is strongly contemporary to our own day, too, isn't it? Are not our *basic* problems today exactly the same that people have always had? Broken relationship with God—sin—is the center and circumference of all our major problems today as it has always been. Maybe this is why in many churches the singing or liturgical use of Psalm 51 would occur in almost every service of worship. What does the psalm say to you, personally, about your own relationship with God?

Confession of Sin

Awareness of sin brings guilt feelings, and the next step to take is to confess sin. It is not by mere chance that the Apostle James urges us to confess sins so that we might find healing. (See James 5:16.) In groups with the holiness tradition we have often found the presence of sin hard to admit; yet if sin is present, it must be confessed before one can get rid of it.

Repression of sin only drives the guilt deeper. It will poison one's attitudes, relationships, disposition. Confess first to God. If more confession was needed, seek out someone who can be trusted with what you have to say. Do not parade the sin; simply admit it humbly. Sometimes this is a matter of dealing with specific transgressions, and they must be faced openly and frankly. With the psalmist it was also a confession that he is human, caught in the drift and current of what the theologians call original sin—the bent of life away from God.

Pray for Forgiveness

At least one-third of the chapter is a prayer asking God's forgiveness and cleansing. We do not have to beg and plead for this; God wants to forgive more than we want it. He takes the initiative in seeking us. The hunger for restoration does not begin with us, but with God. And so simple but earnest and honest prayer, in humility, surrendering everything of past, present, and future, is needed. One must accept by faith the fact that God has forgiven.

Newness of Life

A new life begins when one accepts God's forgiving love. A new heart is created, and the result is new attitudes, relationships, goals, ambitions. One now serves with a sense of stewardship, being responsible for the best use of all one's resources. We walk with joyous steps because all things are made new. We give witness to what God has done. No argument, no cute tricks to get people saved, but we now simply say, This is what God has done for me, and that is the most powerful witness of all.

A Sacrificial Spirit

David knows that all the ritual of religion, all the careful observance of temple procedures, all the offerings of sacrifice cannot take the place of what God really wants. It is the whole of life God wants. Life is now to be lived in obedience to God's will, and one's whole being is given as an offering to God. We cannot buy or purchase what God offers freely—his love, joy, and peace—and that makes the big change in the forgiven life.

Notes on the Biblical Text

"My sin" (51:1-3). The spiritual sensitivity of this writer is reflected in his use of different terms for sin. First he acknowledges transgression, or violation of a known standard. This is conscious rebellion—knowing the way and refusing to walk in it. The second term—iniquity—refers to errors he has committed. Both of these terms as used by the writer—or if used by any of us at times in our lives—could produce a fairly long list of itemized sins. Isn't that true? This third term refers to missing the mark. To miss God's goal for life is sin. Add up all the accumulation of good works; they cannot ever make up for missing what God wants us to become and do. This term is used widely in the New Testament. Are we "hitting the mark" or missing the goal in our lives?

"Wipe away" (51:1-3). Three vivid expressions are used to ask forgiveness. *To wipe away*, or erase, could refer to the priestly function of washing off the tablet on which he had written, and so the prayer is to have "the slate wiped clean." The second, *wash away*, refers to the method used in some parts of the world for washing clothes. The garments are placed in the water and pounded or tread upon until they are clean. The third, *make me clean*, probably means the act of ritual in which the priest, in the Old Testament, would declare one clean. (See Leviticus 13:6.)

"I have sinned against you" (51:4). The hurt and pain and harm done to individuals is bad enough, but in essence sin is rebellion against God. Confession of wrongs done is not as deep as confessing the broken relationship with God, although in many evangelical circles more emphasis is sometimes given to the former.

"From the time I was born" (51:5). The reference is to the natural human bent to evil, not to conception or natural birth.

"Remove my sin" (51:6-9). This is a pre-Christian prayer, a prayer of an ancient Hebrew, and refers to acts in the prescribed ritual before the priest. Small branches of a shrub like an herb were ceremonially dipped in water and used by the priest to sprinkle the water over the penitent sinner.

"Create . . . in me" (51:10-12). The word *create* here is the same word used in Genesis 1, where God created a universe out of chaos. Only God can give this divine renewal. This is an act of divinity, not mere human decision or resolution. A new set of relationships and desires and a way of life are his deepest prayer. With the new creation will come the joy we sing about as "unspeakable and full of glory."

"I will teach" (51:13-15). Toward the end of the prayer comes the vow, the promise, the covenant to witness. Because of God's faithfulness, the psalmist will sing God's praises.

"You do not want sacrifices" (51:16-17). In this unusual insight into the nature of true religion, the psalmist is in harmony with such prophets as Jeremiah, Amos, Hosea, Isaiah, and Micah, as well as the New Testament. This attitude toward the offering of sacrifice to appease God is an abrupt turn in the religious life of the Hebrews. It is a great day for you and me when we realize what God really wants, and we dedicate ourselves to do it.

Some Guidelines for Further Study

Briefly review first the events of David's rise to power as king and then his awful sins and the guilt which followed. Point out that sin can be forgiven, but we cannot stop the influences already set in motion, we cannot undo or unsay, we cannot prevent the consequences of sin no matter if we are forgiven.

Call attention to the three terms used in reference to sin and those asking forgiveness. The real key here is a proper understanding of sin. Basically it is a spiritual matter, though it may involve civil, moral, and ethical matters. Many times we evangelical Christians have made the mistake of thinking of sin as a long list of "dos and don'ts." Sometimes what we have listed in the taboos of religion are rather bad habits, poor taste, errors of judgment. Moral and ethical codes are necessary in society to serve as guidelines for acceptable behavior, but fundamentally sin is between the individual and God.

Restoration begins with God. Call attention to the many New Testament references to a new person, being born again, forming new attitudes and habits.

The fruit of the Spirit cannot grow in the unforgiven or unregenerate heart. True evangelism and faithful witness begin with the forgiven one who has confessed, repented, restored, and now lives in obedience and love.

Chapter 8
Worship as a Solution to Life's Problems
Psalm 73

This is one of the truly great psalms. Nothing in the Old Testament can equal parts of this hymn of faith, especially in its expression of trust, devotion, and piety. It is a record of one person's pilgrimage and intense struggles along the way, from doubt and anxiety to trust and commitment to God. Most of us can identify with this pilgrim's struggles, for many of us have come through the same valleys of doubt. Have we also made our way to a victorious faith?

The psalm begins by stating the conclusion of the pilgrimage. The quest has led to the conviction that no matter how things may appear, God is good and can be trusted.

Why Do the Wicked Prosper?

The big question that bothers this person of so many centuries ago still bothers many of us today. We should note, however, that he is honest in admitting that his own jealousy led him to bitterness. He was standing on a slippery footing and almost lost his relationship with God. It all started, as he says, with jealousy. He was under great tension and pressure; he envied those who seemed to be so successful and who were so godless and arrogant. Are we as honest as he? What is the real source of our doubts?

Certainly this man's struggle is the pilgrimage of most of us. When he refers to the corruption and crookedness of people in places of high influence, the arrogance and pride of many who prosper, the apparent success of those who act as if there is no God, he might be writing a commentary of our own day! Haven't *you* had some of this same struggle? When you see how rampant sin is, how people in high office misuse their trust, when you see people who almost never attend church or identify with righteousness and they seem to get by with their behavior and live well, doesn't this sometimes raise questions in your mind?

This man is disturbed, also, because God's people seem to be "taken in" by these proud, rich, arrogant strutters. Well, he might be talking about us today, for people are still gullible and do not always find their way through the struggle as he did. How many sincere, honest, God-fearing people are easily led astray by the smooth talk of those who seem to speak with authority but are blind leaders of the blind! He is not adverse to wealth and does not curse the rich; he is disturbed by the prosperous who ignore God and live selfishly with ruthless defiance of morality. Some of these are so care-free and continue to increase in wealth even as they continue their injustices and irreligious attitude.

Personal Frustration?

The writer of Psalm 73 is not whining or whimpering, but he does admit to being frustrated. He has lived free from iniquity, a clean and open life before God. But instead of gaining good fortune, he is oppressed with physical suffering that is with him every day.

Remember the Lord's Children

Many of us might parade our bitterness and cynicism before friends and neighbors and thereby perhaps add to our own doubts and misgivings. Not so with the writer of this psalm. He kept silence. He would not shout his complaints where others could hear, for to do so would have made him a traitor to the congregation. That is showing *genuine* concern for other people! How golden was his silence!

Salvation in the Sanctuary

The philosophical problem of why the wicked prosper was not solved. It became more intense, and finally the writer went to the Temple, the place of worship. Going to the house of the Lord for worship is often the necessary first step in solving most of life's perplexities. Here he was able to get values and situations set in their proper perspective. As he worshiped, he began to think of the ultimate outcome and to see things from a new point of view.

This is a new insight, and nothing in the Old Testament surpasses it. Most pre-Christian Hebrews saw death as the end of everything. Here is a new view—not immortality of the soul as we have in the New Testament, but the first sign pointing to it, what has been called a belief in the "afterness" of death. Envy and jealousy are dissipated when one contemplates that so-called prosperity will end at death. The you-can't-take-it-with-you idea was being born. Against the background of death and whatever is after death, the prosperity of the wicked is seen in new perspective. Their reward is temporary; the righteous have a hope eternal, and their peace of mind is not disturbed by envy of that which cannot endure. There is nothing left for one to envy, and a righteous God will act righteously. As the poet now recalls his acute distress and the feeling that there is no moral fairness, he now sees he has acted like a dumb animal, an unthinking beast before God.

Nevertheless

This is one of the great words of human character. How long the list of Bible persons who faced trouble and said, "Nevertheless, I will trust in God!" So it is now. In spite of all the jealousy, doubt, suffering, and pain, he now sees that he can trust his life to the care of God. "Nevertheless" we are together, God has not forsaken me, and I will be guided by his will.

A Praise to God

What is earthly prosperity compared with companionship with the eternal God? Here in the close of the psalm is one of the most profound statements in the Bible. Because of a new outlook, brought by worship and surrender to God, the congregation is urged to witness a new compact and covenant, for "the Lord God omnipotent reigneth" (Rev. 19:6, KJV).

Notes on the Biblical Text

"God is indeed good" (73:1). The opening sentence tells how the song will end. Those with pure hearts will trust in God and not be envious of others.

"I was jealous" (73:2-3). Here is honest testimony. He was slipping and knew it—he was jealous—and confessed the struggle it caused.

"They do not suffer" (73:4-12). It *appears* this way. We see only the tip of the iceberg. We may look at others who *seem* to prosper as they violate all moral, ethical, and spiritual laws. But these outward appearances are deceptive. We never know the inner struggle, turmoil, and turbulence that go on inside a person who disobeys God and conscience. No amount of apparent success can ever equal the peace of mind, the poise, the serenity of the person who is obedient to God and to what he or she knows is God's revealed will, and who keeps his or her own integrity. We have to live forever with *ourselves*—not with what may appear to be unfairness and injustice. The call is to alert us to be sure we do not follow the wrong voices, yield to the subtle temptation to cut corners, go with the crowd, and assume it is right because everybody else is doing it.

"Is it for nothing?" (73:13-14). There is a place for such an honest doubt. God has not said that the obedient would be spared pain or suffering. He has promised to give abundant grace and courage and strength in every situation. As the expression says, "The will of God will not lead you where the grace of God cannot keep you."

"I would not be acting as one of your people" (73:15). He could not forget his obligation to the congregation. There is always somebody whom we cannot let down. Our influence is always to be considered in everything we say and do— just as others have remembered the effect of their actions upon us.

"I went into your Temple" (73: 16-17). Corporate worship is more than going through ritual or form, more than hearing a sermon or enjoying the music or being in fellowship with friends. If we humble ourselves before God in true worship, our perspective will be restored, and our souls cleansed and renewed.

"They are instantly destroyed" (73:18-20). Worldly pleasure and apparent success cannot endure; they bring the horrible end beyond imagination—to have lived in vain.

"I was . . . stupid" (73:21-22). He behaved like an unthinking rhinoceros or hippopotamus—how silly and stupid it was!

"What else do I have . . . but you?" (73:23-28). Companionship with God is most precious. What else can compare with it? This sublime testimony is worthy of the greatest of saints.

Some Guidelines for Further Study

Read the entire psalm together, thoughtfully. Ask for quick responses to the phrases with which we quickly identify.

Spend some time grappling with the *apparent* prosperity of the wicked. List situations from today's world that fit the descriptions given here—in politics, business, education, social living, and even in falsely religious circles. Are we jealous of them?

How much should we do to try to run the universe, and how much should we leave to God's ultimate retribution and rightness? We cannot judge motives, but obvious dishonesty and unethical behavior do come before us daily. How are we to regard them? How easily do we drift with the crowd? The slow but steady erosion of character is just as deadly as a sudden

69

moral failure. How do we avoid the forces of erosion? What are they? How do they affect us in family, business, school, church?

Give some time for witness to this tremendous affirmation in the closing stanzas of the psalm: "God is my strength; he is all I ever need!" Can we say that with honesty?

Chapter 9
Loveliness of God's Dwelling Place
Psalm 84

This is another hymn of pilgrimage with which we modern pilgrims can identify. Some scholars hold that it was written by someone in exile whose fond memories of experiences in the Temple caused him to write this hymn of pathos and religious homesickness. Many others think it was composed by someone who was making his pilgrimage to the Temple and who was overwhelmed with the magnificence of the beauty and loveliness. In any case, the hymn probably was sung by many, many pilgrims as they approached the Temple in Zion.

The first stanza (84:1-4) opens with an exclamation and prayer and tells us at once that the writer is capable of deep spiritual understanding. The hymn stands as the supreme psalm of the sanctuary of God, written by a spiritually sensitive poet.

The Presence of the Living God

Not many buildings erected across the centuries could rival the splendor of the Temple at Jerusalem. As the pilgrim approached it, climbing the hill or mountain, he or she was overwhelmed with emotion at first sight of the Temple and its complex of buildings. Part of this was because of sheer architectural beauty. But this was not all of it. The Temple was seen as the dwelling place of God, and this was what caused the poet's soul to sing. When he was absent from it, his heart yearned for it—not for the building but for the living God who dwelt there.

What of us modern pilgrims? When we go to church, do we go with the sole purpose of worshiping God? We do not look for a God who lives in a building; he lives in our hearts. As Paul told the Corinthians, we are God's temple. (See 1 Corinthians 3:16-17; 6:19-20). Once a man went to the church served by the great Scottish preacher Dr. MacLaren, but he arrived after the worship service had already begun and a minister was preaching. The visitor whispered to the person next to him to ask if the preacher this day was Dr. MacLaren and received this reply, "I don't know who is preaching; I came here to worship God." Well! Why do we go to church? Do we yearn for the presence of God? Do we hunger and thirst for God until we are filled?

Sparrows and Priests

The poet watches birds making nests in the eaves of some buildings and laments that they are more fortunate than he—they are *always* at the Temple. The Levites, who served in various priestly functions, lived in buildings in the Temple area, and they should have always been praising God! Do you think they were? Did their religious activity ever seem routine or monotonous? It is easy to forget the glory and wonder of those first experiences with God following conversion. Do we modern pilgrims ever lose the first love, the sense of the holy, the presence of the divine, because of our easy familiarity with worship?

Anticipation and Preparation

The second stanza (84:5-7) reviews both the hardships of the pilgrimage to Zion and the joy the pilgrim possesses as he looks forward to his arrival.

This was true literally and spiritually. The journey to Jerusalem would be long and tiresome and dangerous. There were mountains to climb and wearisome walks, often without much opportunity for refreshment of food and water. There might be deserts to cross, and there certainly were desolate areas with danger of attack by wild animals or by robbers. It was no easy task to make the annual pilgrimage to Jerusalem. But all of this was forgotten as the pilgrim anticipated the Temple experience.

Does this have a spiritual parallel? Do the anticipations of living a life pleasing to God and the eternal hope and joy overcome the weariness of the journey? Do you recall the song that said, "And the toils of the road will seem nothing when I get to the end of the way?"

This was true for Israel. This nation endured centuries of trouble because of hope for the coming Messiah.

The Renewal and Value of Worship

The third stanza (84:8-12) is filled with poetic imagery and word pictures. The poet tells us how much it meant to him to gather with others at the Temple and bow in worship to God. Nothing he had experienced or even imagined could equal the delight of Temple worship and the spiritual exaltation of being in the presence of God.

It would be better to spend one day at the Temple, if to do so meant he would have to be one of the beggars who gathered near the Temple doors to beg alms, than to live in wealth and comfort and ease away from God's presence. The God whom he adores will bless and keep his obedient children and will not hold back from them any good thing.

Notes on the Biblical Text

"How I love your Temple" (84:1-2). The temple at Jerusalem was a magnificent architectural creation, but the poet is more concerned that this is the dwelling place of God whom he loves

74

and worships. Whether he is an exile in a foreign land or a Hebrew in Palestine, his deepest desire is to worship God.

"Swallows have their own home" (84:3). Birds built nests around the eaves or on top of pillars, and their home was in the physical buildings of the Temple area. The poet also has a home—he is "at home" in worship at God's altar.

"Those who live in your Temple" (84:4). The tribe of Levites, with assigned duties in the Temple, also lived in the area. How fortunate they were!

"How happy are those . . . who . . . make the pilgrimage" (84:5-7). The long pilgrimages to Jerusalem were made each year, and this hymn probably was sung at the Feast of Tabernacles at the start of the new year. In Palestine the rains of October, November, and December bring new life to the parched ground. There the one who trusts in God will find refreshment and renewal in the difficult situations he or she faces. God is trustworthy and will not fail his people.

"Hear my prayer" (84:8-9). Many commentators think these words should be placed at the end of the hymn. It would be sung by the Temple choir as a part of the ritual of prayer for the king. It is likely that the king would be present in Temple worship as God's anointed one, especially at this festival.

"One day spent in your Temple" (84:10). Poetic license would permit some exaggeration, but the figure of speech does indicate the intensity of his feelings and the value he places on Temple worship.

"I would rather stand at the gate" (84:10). There are at least two possible interpretations. One is that this refers to the beggars who stayed near the doors so that they could beg alms from people entering the Temple; the poet says even this would be better than luxurious living away from God. Another point of view suggests that this refers to the guards who monitored the Temple area. These were musicians, doorkeepers, and other attendants. (See 1 Chronicles 26:1-19, for example.) Some have suggested that the psalm is autobiographical, that the writer was an exile and living in luxury away from his early religious training. Now he confesses that nothing has brought him the satisfaction that he remembers he had in the worship at the Temple.

"The Lord is our protector" (84:11). The hymn began on a note of mysticism, but now, in the third stanza, an ethical note is sounded. Like the sun is to the earth, so God is to all humankind. God is the ultimate source of strength, courage, hope, power, and comfort. He is the light of the soul, shelter for the weary, protector for the harassed, and warmth to the faint-hearted. God will not refuse any good thing to those who serve him in obedient love. This is a foreshadow of the Sermon on the Mount, and of such words as these of Paul: "Have no anxiety about anything, but in everything by prayer and supplication with thanksgiving let your requests be made known to God. And the peace of God, which passes all understanding, will keep your hearts and your minds in Christ Jesus" (Philippians 4:6-7, RSV).

"Lord Almighty" (84:12). This is similar to verses 5 and 6, but it seems to be less of a personal testimony and more of an affirmation and call of assurance to his fellow pilgrims.

Some Guidelines for Further Study

In order to understand the place of the Temple in Hebrew worship and the kind of place it was, it would be very helpful to read from a modern-speech translation 1 Kings 5-8 and 1 Chronicles 22-29.

Emphasize that, while this hymn was the expression of one poet, it came into popular usage as a hymn of the Feast of Tabernacles, which coincided with the new year and was a magnificent celebration.

Whether the writer was exiled or not does not change the spiritual application. In either case he was really homesick for the place of worship. Ask for testimonies of any who have had similar experiences—those shut in by illness, people in military service, and others who were denied their customary practice in worship.

The institutional church is criticized as being

ineffective and irrelevant. Are we the cause or cure for that criticism? Are we more concerned about getting large crowds (probably using spectacular methods) or do we assemble in the sanctuary to praise God, study, pray, share mutual concerns, receive instruction and inspiration, enlarge our vision of need and resources, and dedicate ourselves to service?

What preparation do we make for worship? What could we do? What should we do to prepare ourselves for meaningful worship? How do we participate—eagerly? joyously? critically? apathetically?

Chapter 10
Blessings of the One Who Trusts in God
Psalm 91

Among the songs of trust, this psalm stands out as one of the most beautiful and complete. The song sings of victorious and triumphant faith, based on the unshakable conviction that God will protect those who keep their trust in him. Thus it speaks to all people of all times and in all situations; it is surely a hymn for us modern pilgrims. It is always contemporary because it deals with timeless and universal concerns.

Two Difficult Problems

We must not forget we are dealing with poetry, "prayed poems," of a pre-Christian era. Many times in the psalms, or throughout the Old Testament, we must forcefully remind ourselves that Jesus Christ gave new meaning to the concepts and ideas, two of which are found in this psalm.

The writer not only asks but fully expects that God will destroy the wicked or at least place his blessing on their destruction. The writer is to be kept safe and secure, but his enemies will suffer the wrath of God. While it is true that sin carries the seed of death and will ultimately bring destruction, the New Testament lifts up a higher standard of relating to our adversaries. Jesus taught us that God is the final judge of people and that judgment will be executed in the world to come, whereas the psalmist saw immediate destruction as the result of evil living.

A second problem is that the Hebrews had no idea of immortality and made no distinction between God's promise to give spiritual protection and victory and the physical protection for the body. We know today that serving God is no insurance against physical pain or suffering! The genius of the Psalms, however, is that in spite of limitations such as these, they have endured and enriched millions of people across many centuries.

"My God"

The song opens with a shout of joyous praise to God. The relationship between the righteous person and God is tender and intimate. We speak today of having a personal relationship with God, but what could be more personal than the opening stanza of this testimony of faith? How many of us have been inspired by it and strengthened our own weak faith by reading again and again this triumphant affirmation of trust!

The Perils of Life Are Ever with Us

The poet draws heavily on word pictures of situations familiar to the Hebrews as he describes the perils and dangers that beset the pilgrim. The poet feels safe in God's care, although he faces daily all kinds of destructive situations. The unknown traps into which he might fall by accident, or the demons that would torment, or plague or epidemic, or catastrophes in nature will not come near him—God will protect him from them all. Our writer is calm and undisturbed in the midst of turmoil and trouble, for God will not fail him.

This aspect of the psalm, God's protection in the temple or synagogue ritual, was a part of the blessing pronounced by the priest for the lay members of the congregation. Let it be our assurance as we confront our own set of perilous circumstances daily. We can still trust God.

God Promises Help and Protection

The perils have been listed, and now the singer turns to a description of the way God will help the righteous. He believes God's retribution to the ungodly is immediate and awful, but the obedient and faithful have assurance of God's protection. God will sustain him in the hour of great need and will give him victory in all situations and power over all the perils that have been named.

This is the same kind of song that was sung by the poet who could walk through the valley of shadows without fear of being set upon by wild animals, or the poet who sang that God is a mighty fortress, a bulwark never failing.

The promise is that ministering angels of God will stand by to guard, protect, and save him from trouble. The poetic expressions and figures of speech must be heard as "prayed poetry," and we are helped if we do not try to read the psalm as literal prose.

Divine Blessing Is Given

The closing stanza (vv. 14-16) is the priestly blessing, given as a benediction in the name of God. In this role the priest speaks for God to his people, and this would be a high point in the service of worship. It is not merely a man speaking, but a man speaking for the eternal God, the trustworthy One. It is the securing of the covenant relationship between God and the obedient, trusting pilgrim.

Notes on the Biblical Text

"My God" (91:1-2). The relationship is in the first person. Four word pictures are used. To the poet, God is a secret place for hiding, cool shade from the intense heat of the day, a shelter from storm, and a fortress. Two key words (found in the RSV, though not in the TEV) are the verbs *dwell* and *abide*. This relationship of trust is no sudden or spasmodic thing but is built upon permanent and continuing attitudes and habits.

"Safe from all hidden dangers" (91:3). Many versions use a term related to the traps set for catching birds (RSV—"the snare of the fowler"). The trusting person will not get trapped by unwary action or by wandering into trouble.

"Cover you with his wings" (91:4). As the eagle spreads her wings to protect and cover her young, so God will take care of the trusting person.

"You need not fear" (91:5-6). People of surrounding cultures believed strongly in demonology, and this pagan belief has influenced the poet. Some demons, it was thought, would fly into the house at night, giving nightmares or sudden affliction. The daytime demons might have been what we would call sunstroke, a very real possibility for one living in the intense desert heat. The plague might have been any sudden attack of illness that the people of that day would attribute to demons.

"A thousand may fall" (91:7-8). Epidemics of many kinds were far more common then than to many countries of our day. Preventive medicine, better hygiene, vaccines—these have minimized disease of epidemic proportion. Not so in a day thirty centuries or so ago. And, of course, similar conditions exists today in some parts of the world. Although the Hebrew law was very strict on many matters of diet, personal cleanliness, and control of some diseases, the vivid picture of ten thousand persons falling dead is not greatly overdrawn. The error, from the Christian viewpoint, is in assuming that such calamity is visited only on the wicked. We know that no rainstorm, smallpox, germ, or nuclear accident is discriminating—the just and the unjust will both get wet in a thundershower!

"The Lord your defender" (91:9-13). This same thought of immunity from trouble is pursued further, and trouble being viewed still as punishment for sin. The pilgrim in Palestine did not walk on smooth asphalt pavement or concrete sidewalks; the going would be rough and tortuous sometimes. In the midst of danger, however, one has the assurance that in every situation God provides power to overcome.

"God says, 'I will save those who love me' " (91:14-16). Here is an abrupt change in the poem. This passage would be spoken by the priest in charge of the worship. It is more than a gesture of goodwill or a benediction. The priest speaks on behalf of God and in his name. The blessing is a promise made on behalf of God. God will impart salvation to the obedient follower, although today we know that salvation must be seen in its broadest—and eternal—sense. What is promised is not aspirin for a headache, but serenity, poise, power, and peace, even in circumstances that frustrate and bring pain, suffering and fear. We gain most help from the psalms when we fill their forms full of

84

the content of the teachings of Jesus—then they are unsurpassed in the expression of the soul in divine worship.

Some Guidelines for Further Study

Remind the group we are dealing with ancient poetry, pre-Christian by a few centuries, and are using imagery common to the Hebrew people though not always familiar to us. The center and core of this psalm is that God honors the one who humbly trusts him and who follows in obedience; he will give strength, courage, hope, and overcoming power. That affirmation is timeless, though illustrations may vary from one culture to another.

As you reflect upon and explain the perils that are listed, you could get the group to call to mind some of the perils faced by the modern pilgrim who seeks to obey God. What are some of them?

We must be honest in dealing with this matter of God's protection. One bypath you could easily take leads you into fatalism—whatever will happen will occur no matter what you do. Thousands of people believe this, yet it is not Christian. You could also follow the road that makes magic out of religion; some people do. Can we sincerely pray for God to deflect bullets and bombs of warfare so that a few choice people are spared? Can we honestly ask God to protect us on the highway if we drive carelessly, at unreasonably high speed, in cars that are imperfect, or when we are suffering from fatigue or are extremely sleepy? Isn't it more Christian to pray that we may act with good sense?

Give time for some exchange of personal experiences of trust, times when we felt the confirmation of this psalm and God provided interior security and adequate resources to see us through. We sometimes say we are doing all right "under the circumstances," as someone has aptly said; this psalm calls us to get out from under the circumstances and stand on top of them, victoriously praising God for his steadfast love.

Chapter 11
A Hymn of Thanksgiving
Psalm 103

Many of us have committed this psalm to memory. It is one of the outstanding hymns of personal devotion in all literature. The poet has suffered pain and guilt and has come close to death. He has been in the valleys of dark shadows and on the sunlit mountain. He sings of God's redeeming love in all situations.

Summons to the Soul

As if he were speaking to another person, the poet calls upon his own soul to praise the Lord. In a spontaneous outburst of praise he marvels with awe and reverence that all he is and has he owes to a gracious and redemptive God. In Hebrew thought the idea of God's judgment usually prevailed, but here judgment and mercy meet in redemptive love. This is a broad hint of what Jesus made so clear: that although God is righteous and cannot but hate sin, he also takes the initiative in showing mercy in redemption.

God's Kind Dealings with a Man

The poet sings a personal testimony in public worship as he recounts the way God has

blessed his life. He was in sin but was now forgiven. He was sick and was now well. He suffered some very serious illness, came close to
death, but was healed by God. He not only
speaks in past tense but affirms that this is the
way God deals with one always.

To redeem is to buy back again. In modern
terms, one can borrow money from the pawn
broker, giving in pledge an item of greater
value. To get the item back again, one repays
the loan with interest, or "redeems" it. In centuries past the term was used in regard to the
purchase of slaves. So the poet is indebted to
God for having done something costly to rescue
him from the pit. The pit could refer to the
realm of evil into which he had fallen.

He is treated royally, but the crown he wears
is God's kindness and mercy, not the jeweled
crown of a king. God also provides what the
poet needs, and his life is under the constant
process of renewal. What a testimony!

God's Mercy and Judgment with Israel

The hymn of praise is now expanded from
the personal to a witness of how God has
blessed Israel. He goes as far back as Moses in
reminding Israel of the way God has led them
and dealt with them patiently and graciously.

Through the years God did not deal as
harshly with the Israelites as they often
deserved—nor does he with you and me. He is

just, but his justice has always been full of mercy. This keen insight of the poet had often been lost to the Hebrews, even though the prophets tried so hard to proclaim it.

How can we comprehend the magnitude of God's mercy and love? It is as far removed from our human understanding as the sky is from the earth. His forgiveness to Israel has been so complete that he has separated their guilt from him as far as one horizon is from another. Finally, the relationship between God and Israel is like that of father to children, a concept most fully demonstrated by Jesus.

God's Strong Mercy to Frail Humankind

This stanza of the hymn (vv. 15-18) is not unlike Psalm 90 in which the weakness of humankind is the background against which the greatness of God is pictured. In this stanza, the hymn has moved from Israel to focus on all humankind. God's love is overwhelming in the light of human frailty and helplessness. All people are as fragile as a wild flower, made of mere dust, and are no more permanent than the grass in the fields.

But to these frail creatures the eternal God has extended his love and care, with the provision that it is given to those who hear the word of the Lord and follow in humble obedience. All of our humanness and weakness can be turned to strength when we live in obedience to God.

Glory to God in the Highest

The poet has begun with his own experiences and blessings, expanded to include Israel. He then moves to include all humankind. In this stanza (vv. 19-22) the hymn calls on all the hosts of heaven to join in praise and joyous celebration. He calls for praise from the heavenly servants—sun, moon, stars, planets, angels—to include the whole universe. Nothing is left out. All that God has created are invited to join this triumphant anthem.

We are reminded of the moving, stirring, rolling "Hallelujah Chorus" of Handel's *Messiah* as we read this stanza and imagine what such an anthem of praise would sound like. The buildup is almost unbearable as chorus joins chorus and the volume and intensity increase.

Finally, the poet calls upon his own soul to join the anthem, and we hear his voice added to the swelling chorus of praise. As he began, so he closes, "Bless the Lord, O my soul!"

Notes on the Biblical Text

"Praise the Lord" (103:1). The term suggests that one is bowing on bended knees in adoration and worship, a custom used to honor royalty.

"All my being" (103:1). The song must come from the soul, not just from the lips.

"How kind he is" (103:2). Many versions say "forget not his dealings." How *easily* we forget the millions of ways in which God has shown his love and care.

"He forgives" (103:3). This is a personal testimony. We do not know what sins are on the record, but the poet knows they are all forgiven.

"He . . . heals" (103:3). The personal witness continues to include healing of the body.

"He keeps me" (103:4). At some time the writer had been very close to death, and only through the mercy of God was he brought back to life.

"He . . . blesses me" (103:4). Many versions use *redeemed* as the verb. God has paid whatever price was necessary to completely restore the psalmist to wholeness. So he does with you and me.

"Like an eagle" (103:5). An eagle does not remain young, but it appears to. At the molting season it sheds its old feathers and new ones appear. It is renewed in appearance and in vigor and strength. The psalmist testifies that God provides renewal—and you and I know how true it is!

"He revealed his plans to Moses" (103:6-7). This is a direct reference to Exodus 34:1-7 where Moses met God on Mount Sinai and received the Ten Commandments. The remarkable thing is not how God wrote on the tablets, but his self-revealing as detailed in verses 5-6 of the Exodus passage. God has not failed to be and do what he promised Moses centuries ago, for that is the essence of God eternally. Mercy and love are not what God *has* but a part of what he *is*.

"The Lord is merciful" (103:8-10). Israel's sins deserved the wrath and anger of God, just as ours do. God did not deal with Israel as they deserved, but according to his very nature. What he *does* is the extension and the expression of what he *is*. Read in this connection such passages as Isaiah 57:16 and Jeremiah 3:5, 12.

"As high as the sky" (103:11). The extent of God's love is limitless, beyond our poor power to comprehend.

"As far as the east is from the west" (103:12). Forgiveness is not partial or conditional or temporary. In poetic imagery, as far as one can see or imagine from one horizon to the other, so far does God remove sin. Has this happened to you? If so, you have something to sing about, just as this poet says.

"As a father is kind" (103:13-14). Contrast the strength of a powerful and loving, kind, tender father with the frailty and weakness of a child. Jesus developed this figure of speech more fully to show us the strength and the concern of God's redemptive love.

"As for us" (103:15-16). By contrast to the temporary and vulnerable nature of humans, the love of God endures, moving on to include every new generation. As Paul says in his famous passage on love, it will outlast anything. And it does. This promise is not restricted to Israel, but it is for everyone who lives in faith and obedience. See Isaiah 55:6-11.

"He is king over all" (103:19). This refers not only to the supremacy of God, but it is a glimpse into the real nature of the kingdom of God. That kingdom is not a future event or happening, but it is here and now in the hearts of those who crown him king and Lord and live in obedience.

"Praise the Lord" (103:20-22). This call to join the anthem is universal, expressing the highest joy and exultation one can imagine. Can you imagine what that chorus sounds like?

Some Guidelines for Further Study

Most of those in your group will be very familiar with this psalm. They have used it in weddings, funerals, in worship, in private and public devotion. You could read it aloud, in concert, or responsively.

How old is the message that God heals our bodies, a doctrine exploited by fanatics, but still a reality? Many individuals can give personal witness, as can the writer of this page!

Even more marvelous than physical healing is the forgiveness of sin. The key is surrender of everything to God. We must also forgive ourselves and one another. This forgiveness is never cheap or easy; it cost God his Son on Calvary. Ask if all of us have forgiven those who have trespassed against us, so that with pure hearts we can receive God's forgiveness.

If you can sing without disturbing others, close the session by singing the doxology, "Praise God from Whom All Blessings Flow."

Chapter 12
God's Word As Light and Life

Psalm 119

A Most Unusual Composition

Our English translations lose the unique characteristic of the form of Psalm 119. Most of them show stanzas of eight lines each, which is correct. But what we may not recognize is that the psalm is in the form of an *acrostic*. Each stanza begins with a letter of the twenty-two-letter Hebrew alphabet in proper sequence. In each stanza, all eight lines begin with the same letter. Just try preserving that structure in an English translation and at the same time keeping integrity with the meaning and the poetic expression!

What Is the Law?

Law itself, as used here, really means guidance, direction, or instruction. We do not know for certain whether the writer uses the term *law* to mean the Pentateuch (first five books of the Bible) or whether he meant all the books of the Law and the Prophets.

Just as each stanza has eight verses, or lines, so eight different words are used for the Law. Of these eight, four refer to strictly legal commands or prohibitions—*precepts, statutes, commandments, ordinances*. The other four are *testimonies*, God's witness to his will; *word*, the voice of God; *way*, the path the pilgrim follows through life's complexities; and *law*, or instruction.

Party Differences

The writer clearly recognizes two major parties in the Hebrew community. There were the proud, arrogant, and wicked people who have complete disregard for God and their spiritual and moral heritage, living for their own desires. The others, with which the psalm writer is identified, are devout, godly, loyal, humble people who try honestly to please God and who appreciate their natural heritage. These differences have existed through the centuries.

Inspiration of the Law

One theme runs through all 176 verses of this psalm, and that is praise of God's law. The psalmist does not find it burdensome. He is not annoyed by it. He delights in it. The Law inspires him beyond his ability to express. In the Law he finds his greatest joy. In the midst of trouble, adversity, misunderstanding, and difficulties of every kind, he is held secure and firm in his commitment to God and in obedience to his word.

Obedience Is a Joy

Since the Law is the same creative word that spoke humanity and the universe into existence, it is perfect and assures one of God's presence. The Law is obeyed because it is of God and it is true and just, not because of a sense of duty. The Law is a reminder of God's justice, but it is also the assurance of hope, peace, and true liberty.

The only way the Law can be fully obeyed is for one to center his or her whole being in the will of God. Appreciating or delighting in the Law is not enough; it requires obedience. The writer admits that he strays from the path, but even in his wandering the Law is ever with him and draws him back to obedience.

Those in the community who are not devoted to the Law will hold it in contempt. They will persecute the one who tries to live obediently and in their arrogant pride will see themselves as being above the Law. So God's constant presence and support are sorely needed to hold him steadfast and true amidst his enemies. God will provide a means of escape from or victory over his enemies and their harassment.

The heart of the writer is like a fountain, bubbling forth with joy and sheer spiritual delight. He believes that God is creator and sustainer of the universe and will uphold the obedient righteous.

Notes on the Biblical Text

This psalm is so long that all we can do here in this brief space is to indicate the content of each stanza by a title and a few words of commentary. (The titles suggested here are not always those given in Today's English Version.)

"Happiness of the Blameless Life" (119:1-8). The poet's deepest desire is that he may live a life consistent with God's law and that he will always be blameless and above shame.

"How Is Life Kept Clean?" (119:9-16). Temptations to do evil abound, but the poet has determined to live obediently before God. He has memorized much of the Law and often quotes it from memory to strengthen his commitment.

"A Prayer for Illumination" (119:17-24). He is a pilgrim (so are we!) and needs illumination on his path so that he will not go astray. In the midst of persecution by proud and insolent people, he is strengthened by the law of God.

"Walking in the Right Path" (119:25-32). Having received forgiveness, the poet asks God to teach him obedience. He eagerly asks for greater understanding.

"Obedience Is Its Own Reward" (119:33-40). The religious have always hoped reward for right living, but we are sometimes mistaken about the reward. The inner satisfaction of obedience is reward enough.

"The Law Brings Freedom" (119:41-48).

Instead of the Law's being inhibiting or restrict-
ing, it gives the poet a freer and fuller life.
Because of this larger life, he will proclaim his
testimony with justifiable pride.

"The Singing Pilgrim" (119:49-56). Time on
earth is short at its best, and the poet is a pilgrim with no permanent abiding place here.
Wherever he is and in whatever circumstances,
his religion breaks forth in song.

"Considering God's Way and Then Following" (119:57-64). The poet sings of the all-
sufficiency of God's law.

"Learning through Adversity" (119:65-72).
He accepts affliction as God's discipline; this has
led him to new commitment to obedience.

"Affliction May Mean Discipline" (119:73-80).
He is resigned to affliction and adversity. He
will remain steadfastly loyal.

"Faithful though Persecuted" (119:81-88). His
persecution must have been fierce and intense,
but his commitment to obedience does not
waver though rescue seems long in coming.

"The Law Has Been a Sustainer" (119:89-96).
The Law has been the source of his strength.
Persecuted to the point of death, he affirms
that God's word is the one surety.

"Wisdom Is Greater Than Knowledge"
(119:97-104). The Law exceeds the ability of
teachers in giving insight, discernment, and
wisdom which go beyond mere knowledge.

"A Lamp and a Light" (119:105-112). The

Law lights the dark road for the obedient pilgrim and makes clear each step along the way.

"Safe in God's Law" (119:113-120). Safety can be found only in God. God's awesome power will rescue the faithful and punish the wicked.

"Holding to God's Promise" (119:121-128). He longs for God's mercy and vindication; he wishes God would act now. Nevertheless, he holds faithfully to God's commandments.

"The Law Gives Guidance when Understood" (119:129-136). He wholeheartedly embraces all God's teaching and grieves that not everyone does so.

"God Is Eternally Right" (119:137-144). The Law is not arbitrary or whimsical, but it issues from God's essential nature and his unchanging rightness.

"Always in Prayer and Meditation" (119:145-152). Early in the morning the psalmist joins others in worship, and in the night he meditates on the Law, constantly hunger for righteousness.

"Distressed but not Dismayed" (119:153-160). Because he has been true to the Law, he has the right to plead for rescue. The wicked will not be saved, but he asks to be saved because he has been obedient.

"A Wonderful Way out of Trouble" (119:161-168). He patiently awaits deliverance while obeying the Law. Seven times each day he expresses his gratitude. The number seven symbolized completeness or perfection. His gratitude is, thus, constant, complete.

"A Fountain Bubbling with Praise" (119:169-176). He asks for life in order to continue to praise God's justice.

Some Guidelines for Further Study

The passage is too long to read in your group; you will do well just to cover the nature of the Hebrew composition, the central theme, and the titles of the twenty-two stanzas. How do we regard the Word of God? Do we *study* it? Do we know its central message? Do we use it to support our own notions or do we read with open minds to let it speak to our needs and bring fresh insights? Do we regard it as a list of commands or restrictions, or as a record of God's self-revelation and of our response? Do we read the Bible to find instruction, hope, inspiration, and guidance for daily living? Committing ourselves to study God's Word as faithfully as did the psalmist brings rewards beyond expression. Class members may wish to testify how God's Word has permitted them to sing in the night.

Chapter 13
A Song of Ascent
Psalm 130

The title "Songs of Ascent" is given to a group of psalms (120-134) that were likely chanted or sung by the Hebrew pilgrims making their way to worship in the Jerusalem temple, or in later years as they approached the synagogue for worship. Psalm 130 may have been one of the penitential hymns that the pilgrims sang as they ascended from the valley to Mount Zion. Spiritually also, the poet rises from the depths of despair to hope and solid trust. This psalm is usually understood to have four stanzas: let us look briefly at each of them.

A Prayer of Desperation

The psalmist is in the depths of despair. We are not told the cause, although reference to forgiveness might suggest deep guilt.

The poet has fallen into a deep abyss; all of us modern pilgrims can quickly identify with him as did many Hebrews who later chanted his hymn. He may have been physically ill and near death. It could have been an emotional depression out of which he saw no ray of hope or light. It could have been intense guilt, growing out of his awareness of unforgiven sin. He was at the bottom of the hole, the end of his rope, in the darkest of dark nights. He had been abandoned and was helpless.

Out of this deep depression he turned to God in prayer. Everything seemed hopeless, and yet he still believed in God. The prayer is a cry of anguish and urgency. He did not have to bear his burden alone, and so he did what we always ought to do—he prayed. Did not Jesus tell us, centuries later, that instead of fainting in dire distress we ought always to pray? The person who has lived close to God when things are going smoothly will be able to pray when the situation seems utterly hopeless.

In God There Is Forgiveness (vv. 3-4)

In the second stanza the poet looked around him and was aware that all humankind is caught in the web of sinfulness, a sort of unity through common guilt. Estrangement from God is common to all of us. His text could well be, "All have sinned and fall short of the glory of God" (Romans 3:23, RSV).

God does not add up these sins to hold against us, for his very nature is to forgive. This redemptive love that issues in forgiveness stands in sharp contrast to the wayward pilgrim who wanders into sin. Sin seems the worse when viewed against the holiness of God; we stand in reverence and awe before this holy

God who holds out forgiveness toward everyone who will accept it.

Only in the depths of one's guilt can one begin to perceive the height, length, breadth, and extent of God's forgiving love.

The Man in Despair Waits in Hope
(vv. 5-6)

Now we come to the third stanza of this hymn, which echoes Isaiah 40:31—"They that wait upon the Lord shall renew their strength."

For the poet the night is still here, but morning is on the way. Perhaps he paces back and forth impatiently, but also in confidence that the word of forgiveness will come and dawn will end the long night of depression and despair. As a watchman at the city wall waits for morning light, so the poet waits for divine assurance that he has been forgiven. We understand, of course, that this message foretells the New Testament message of salvation by faith. This psalm causes us to think of some of Paul's statements about guilt, depression, confession, prayer, and the acceptance of God's forgiveness.

A Call to the Worshiping Congregation
(vv. 7-8)

The final stanza is the call to all of Israel to wait upon the Lord to experience his acts of redemptive love. Because of his own despair, he knows how other sufferers long for healing. The deep darkness of the soul leads one to think of others who also feel guilt and remorse and pray for their salvation. Martin Luther once said that one "cannot know what hope is who has never been in the midst of trials and temptations." One who has been there will not only feel empathy for others but will urge them to turn to God in expectant prayer, waiting for his sure word of deliverance.

So the man in the pit of despair in the first stanza becomes teacher and preacher in the closing stanza. His faith is firm that God will not only answer his own prayer, but will hear the prayer of all Israel when it is in the spirit of humility, contrition, confession, earnestness, and expectancy. The song closes on this great affirmation of faith.

Notes on the Biblical Text

"Out of the depths" (130:1). This expression (from the KJV) is not uncommon in the Old Testament. It means, literally, almost submerged in deep water, such as a lake or sea, and is used as a synonym for acute distress or death itself.

"Hear my cry" (130:2). When all seems hopeless and lost, when in deep adversity, as the song says, "Where could I go but to the Lord." This is the same keen agony that, in deeper intensity, caused Jesus to pray in Gethsemane, "If it be possible, let this cup pass," and to cry on the cross, "Why hast thou forsaken me?" We are encouraged by the Word of God to call upon him for help; this is the right and proper thing to do in time of adverse circumstances.

"If you kept a record of our sins" (130:3). God is not a divine bookkeeper, carefully recording all wrongdoing. He knows our sins, and we know them. But we are more likely to remember them than he is! We are the ones with guilt who can find no hiding place for sin. If God did keep such a record, who would be blameless? Whose name would not be on the list? All humankind would stand guilty before God.

"You forgive us" (130:4). The essence of God is forgiveness and redemptive love. We think we take the initiative in calling for help, but our cry is only an echo of God's efforts to reconcile us to himself. Long before God's plan of redemption was fully completed and revealed in the life, death, and resurrection of Jesus Christ, people knew that God is the one who forgives sin.

"That thou mayest be feared" (130:4, KJV). The word *fear* in God's presence appears often in the Bible. It does not mean to be frightened or scared. In the presence of the holy one of Israel, the sinner is overwhelmed with awe, wonder, trust, thankfulness, and love. Perhaps *reverence* is a word that comes close to the meaning of fear as it is used here. This attitude of reverence and gratitude will cause us to remember our shortcomings and to serve the

Lord gladly. What law cannot force us to do, the love of God persuades us to do with joy. It may be the same reaction a budding artist, a student, has in the presence of a master artist—ashamed of one's own poor work but lured by the temptation to excellence and striving to perfect one's work.

"I wait eagerly" (130:5-6). There are many ways to wait. We can wait for a bus or plane that is later than expected and be filled with anxiety and irritation. Why is it late? When will it arrive? Was there an accident? What will this do to other plans I have made? So the anxiety builds. One can wait without hope. A prisoner under sentence of death waits—day after day—but with no hope of pardon, spending each hour in anguish of the slow passing of time.

We can wait, knowing a promise will be kept. When a loved one says he or she will be home for Christmas, we wait in trust. So the poet waits for God's help. He knows it will come. His longing is intense, but he has hope. As the night watchmen guard the palace gates or the city wall, they know dawn will come and the day shift will take over. They wait with confidence.

"Israel, trust in the Lord" (130:7-8). The poet calls the whole community to a new commitment. What God does for one, he can do for the nation. God will keep faith with his covenant people.

Some Guidelines for Further Study

Martin Luther liked Psalms 51 and 130 best; they foreshadow the Christian teaching of salvation by faith.

In the afternoon, before his famous Aldersgate heartwarming evening, John Wesley went to St. Paul's church in London and was deeply moved as he listened to the choir sing Psalm 130. It was God's preparation for what was to follow! Could that happen to us? Could renewal of the spirit follow the steps outlined in Psalm 130?

Everybody can identify with this psalm. You could let a few people relate some of their experiences of being "in the depths" and of how they turned to God for help and were delivered.

You might discuss the kinds of "depths" common to us today. Also, how do we wait upon the Lord? With what faith do we pray?

There are implications for the group also. The family, the community, the church of your congregation, the nation—all of these groups have the "depth of despair" experience at times, and our happy assignment is to carry the good news that God does hear prayer and will answer.